THROUGH THE EYES

—— OF A ——

LION

FACING IMPOSSIBLE PAIN
FINDING INCREDIBLE POWER

—— THE BIBLE STUDY ——

LEVI LUSKO

Lifeway Press®
Nashville, Tennessee

EDITORIAL TEAM

Susan Hill
Writer

Reid Patton
Content Editor

Jon Rodda
Art Director

Joel Polk
Editorial Team Leader

Brian Daniel
Manager, Adult Discipleship

Brandon Hiltibidal
Director, Adult Ministry

Ben Mandrell
President, Lifeway Christian Resources

Published by Lifeway Press® • © 2021 Levi Lukso

No part of this book may be reproduced or transmitted in any form or by any means, electronic or mechanical, including photocopying and recording, or by any information storage or retrieval system, except as may be expressly permitted in writing by the publisher. Requests for permission should be addressed in writing to Lifeway Press®; One Lifeway Plaza; Nashville, TN 37234.

ISBN 978-1-0877-2822-3 • Item Number 005828822

DEWEY: 234.2

Subject Headings:: HOPE / FAITH / CHRISTIAN LIFE

To order additional copies of this resource, write to Lifeway Resources Customer Service; One Lifeway Plaza; Nashville, TN 37234; fax 615-251-5933; call toll free 800-458-2772; order online at Lifeway.com; or email orderentry@lifeway.com.

Printed in the United States of America

Adult Ministry Publishing • Lifeway Resources • One Lifeway Plaza • Nashville, TN 37234

CONTENTS

ABOUT THE AUTHOR

Levi Lusko is the founder and lead pastor of Fresh Life Church, located in Montana, Wyoming, Oregon, and Utah. He is the best-selling author of *Through the Eyes of a Lion, Swipe Right,* and *I Declare War.* Levi also travels the world speaking about Jesus. He and his wife, Jennie, have one son, Lennox, and four daughters: Alivia, Daisy, Clover, and Lenya, who is in heaven.

INTRODUCTION

One of the greatest military deceptions that has ever taken place happened in the battle of Normandy on D-Day. Soldiers rained down, and boats arrived all along the coast of France as we strategized to take it back from Hitler's clutches. Troops had to fool the Nazis into believing that Normandy was not the site we were going to invade and that the allied forces were actually coming in from the south of France. Mannequins hooked up to parachutes, and inflatable tanks were deployed all along the south of France to make Hitler's army believe that was the site of the invasion while U.S. troops snuck into Normandy. That day is often compared to the Trojan Horse incident—where a horse was taken into a city and unbeknownst to those in the city—it was full of soldiers.

In a similar way, I believe when God allows difficulty into your life, it's actually a Trojan horse, and He is setting you up in the midst of hard circumstances so you can be a part of Him saving many lives. And that is essentially what you're going to discover in this six-session Bible study called *Through the Eyes of a Lion*. If you can learn to think and see differently—you'll be able to live beautifully and powerfully.

HOW TO USE THIS STUDY

This Bible study book includes six weeks of content for group and personal study.

GROUP SESSIONS

Regardless of what day of the week your group meets, each session of content begins with the group session. Each group session uses the following format to facilitate simple yet meaningful interaction among group members and with the truths of God's Word presented in this study.

> **START.** This page includes questions to get the conversation started and to introduce the video teaching.

> **WATCH.** This page provides space to take notes on the video teaching.

> **DISCUSS.** This page includes questions and statements that guide the group to respond to Levi's video teaching and to explore relevant Bible passages.

PERSONAL STUDY

PERSONAL STUDY. Each session provides two personal Bible studies. Each personal study works through the Scriptures to deepen their understanding of the week's topic. Each study includes questions and teaching designed to help participants understand the Bible and apply its teaching to their lives.

BIBLE READING PLAN. Additionally, each week of personal study provides four guided Bible readings that allow you to read related passages from the Scripture and learn to study them on your own. Each reading follows the SOAP method, outlined on the next page.

THE SOAP METHOD

How To S.O.A.P.

S - SCRIPTURE

Open your Bible to your reading for the day. Take time reading and allow God to speak to you. When you are done, look for a verse that particularly spoke to you that day, and write it in your journal.

O - OBSERVATION

What struck you and caught your attention in what you read? What do you think God is saying to you in this Scripture? Ask the Holy Spirit to teach you and reveal Jesus to you. Paraphrase and write this Scripture down in your own words.

A - APPLICATION

Personalize what you have read by asking yourself how it applies to your life right now. Perhaps it is instruction, encouragement, a new promise, or correction for a particular area of your life. Write how this Scripture can apply to you today.

P - PRAYER

This can be as simple as asking God to help you use this Scripture, or even a prayer for a greater insight on what He may be revealing to you. Remember, prayer is a two-way conversation, so be sure to listen to what God has to say. Now, write it out.

———

*We don't have to wait until we get to
heaven to live in the light of God's goodness.
It's available to us here and now through Jesus.*

———

WEEK 1

TURN OFF
THE DARK

START

Welcome to Session 1.

If you've ever traveled on a pitch-black road in the dead of night, you know how daunting darkness can be. Every twist and turn in the road represents the unknown and fear of what might be around the corner. When we don't know what's ahead, it's tempting to imagine the worst-case scenario. But it doesn't take much light to make a path out of the darkness. Even a dim light in the distance can give us hope and provide a path out of the darkness.

Why do you think so many children are afraid of the dark? Were you scared of the dark when you were young? If so, how did you cope with your fear?

Why are we prone to imagine the worst when we don't know what's ahead?

What comes to mind when you hear the terms "light and darkness"?

Creating light was God's first priority in the creation account (Gen. 1:3). The theme of light and darkness originates in the Book of Genesis and is woven throughout the Bible. The Scriptures contrast light and darkness to describe spiritual realities. Spiritually speaking, light and darkness represent the differences between good and evil, truth and lies, righteousness, and wickedness.

Pray and ask God to use our time together.
After praying, watch the video teaching.

WATCH

Video sessions available at Lifeway.com/Lion or with a subscription to SmallGroup.com

DISCUSS

1. Levi opened the video by discussing the parable Jesus told in Matthew 7:24-27 about the difference between foundations built on rock versus sand. How is it possible to have the appearance of a solid foundation and, in reality, be on the verge of collapsing? What does it means to build your life on a solid foundation?

2. Levi shared the story of his daughter Lenya's celebration of life just before Christmas. The death of a child is the most excruciating experience a parent can go through. But Levi said, "We were equipped when the darkness came." How did his foundation in Jesus guide him out of the darkness?

3. Share about a time when you were caught off guard by dark circumstances. What happened? How did you respond?

4. Storms come in a variety of circumstances. What is one lesson you've learned from your storms? How did that experience shape your faith?

5. How would you describe your relationship with Jesus in your current season of life? What areas of your relationship with Jesus would you like to focus on in the coming weeks?

6. Where do you need Jesus' help to "turn off the dark" for you?

Close your discussion with prayer. Remind those in your group to complete the personal studies and Bible reading over the next week.

PERSONAL STUDY 1
LIGHT IN THE DARKNESS

One thing all people have in common is a desire to be happy. God wired human beings with a desire for joy and fulfillment. Have you ever met someone who hasn't pursued happiness? Me neither. But it doesn't take long to realize this world is filled with pitfalls that can derail happiness. Evidence of darkness is everywhere we look, and we even see it in our own lives. Maybe it's in the form of loneliness, fear, depression, or guilt. Deep down, we know things aren't the way they are supposed to be, but we don't know how to fix it. Thankfully, in His mercy, God sent light into the darkness.

Read John 1:1-18.

How many times is "light" referred to in this passage?
What or Whom is the light referring to?

The opening verses in John's Gospel are known as the prologue, and this passage is one of the most informative accounts of Jesus' coming. Right away, the apostle John reveals that Jesus is more than a teacher or a prophet— Jesus is God (John 1:1,14), and He is the source of all light.

TURN OFF THE DARK

"In Him was life, and the life was the light of men."
JOHN 1:4

With the above passages in mind, what are some ways in which Jesus shines a light into the darkness?

In Scripture, the words "light" and "life" are often referred to as the opposite of "death" and "darkness." Metaphorically, death and darkness refer to sin and its effects on the world. Jesus came to shine light in the darkness—to turn off the dark. Since Jesus is all-powerful, He could've done this in any manner of His choosing. Certainly, Jesus could've shined His light from a distance, and it would've been powerful enough to reach us, but that's not what He did. He made the choice to come to us.

THE LIGHT OF IMMANUEL

Read Matthew 1:23.

Did you catch that? Immanuel means "God with us." Jesus entered into this dark world because He wanted to be with us. He isn't distant or aloof. Jesus willingly took on flesh. In doing so, Jesus entered into our pain and suffering with the intention of being present with us and shining a light in the dark cracks and crevices of our lives.

**Look up the following passages and write down
what they teach about light and darkness.**

John 8:12

Acts 26:16-18

1 John 1:5

1 John 1:7

1 Thessalonians 5:5

Psalm 119:105

Which of these passages spoke most directly to you?

Which of these Scriptures address your current circumstances?

Because Jesus came to earth and took on the form of a man, He can sympathize with our sins, sufferings, and weaknesses (Heb. 4:14-15). Jesus understands the hardships of being a human being, and He has compassion for us. Jesus not only understands our plight—He makes Himself entirely approachable and available to help. Consider this invitation from the Book of Hebrews.

Let us therefore come boldly to the throne of grace, that we
may obtain mercy and find grace to help in time of need.
HEBREWS 4:16

On a scale of 1-10, how mindful are you of the reality that Jesus is approachable and willing to grant grace and mercy?

In what specific areas do you need God's grace right now? What prevents you from asking God for help?

THE LIGHT THAT DESTROYS DEATH

It's one thing to believe that Jesus can shine light into darkness and eradicate things like loneliness, fear, despair, and guilt. But what about when we are grieving the death of a loved one? Or what if we fear death ourselves? Paul addressed this topic in a letter to Timothy, his younger understudy. Paul wrote

Jesus Christ [...] has abolished death and brought life
and immortality to light through the gospel.
2 TIMOTHY 1:10

Jesus came to turn off the darkness of death by turning on the light. Hebrews 2:15 says Jesus came to "release those who through fear of death were all their lifetime subject to bondage." The incarnation came before the resurrection—so we could live with hope and die without fear. Paul wrote:

> *O Death, where is your sting?*
> *O Hades, where is your victory?*
> 1 CORINTHIANS 15:55

How does the hope we have in Jesus diminish the sting of death?

Being a Christian doesn't mean we won't grieve the loss of loved ones, but why can Christians grieve with hope?

How does the ability to grieve with hope make Christianity distinct?

NO FEAR OF THE DARK

This is the gospel: Jesus turned off the dark. Death has been stripped of its power (Col. 2:15). Instead of being fearful, we can look at death victoriously. This is what Paul meant when he wrote Jesus abolished death. He shines a light into our dark places. We don't have to wait until we get to heaven to live in the light of God's goodness. It's available to us here and now through Jesus.

End your time today praying that Jesus will shine
a light in the areas you need Him.

PERSONAL STUDY 2

PREPARED FOR DARKNESS

Sooner or later, we all experience seasons of hardship and difficulty. If you're not currently facing adversity, now is an excellent time to prepare yourself and get grounded in your faith, so you're ready when it comes. Hardships come in many shapes and forms; sickness, divorce, financial problems, family issues, and anxiety are common offenders. When we're struggling, it often feels like the adversity will never end. We can't avoid the hard things in life, but if we're prepared, we can manage them much more effectively.

ROCK OR SAND?

Read Matthew 7:24-27.

In this parable, Jesus tells the story of two men who had the same goal—each of them planned to build a house. By outward appearances, both houses looked sturdy. But upon closer examination, one house was built on rock and the other on sand. When the storm hit, one house was demolished because of its poor foundation, while the other weathered the storm and survived intact. Jesus taught that the difference maker between the two men is that one heard Jesus' words and did them (v. 24). Obedience creates a firm foundation to build our lives upon.

Why is being obedient to God's Word essential for building your life on a solid foundation?

Why is it crucial to know and understand the promises of God before being confronted with a crisis?

RECOGNIZING THE LIGHT

To obey Jesus and build a strong foundation, we have to develop the ability to hear from Him. In the middle of hardship, it's easy to lose your bearings. When you're suffering, everything feels amplified, and it can be challenging to know who or what to believe. That's why it is crucial to have the kind of relationship with Jesus that's so intimate you can pick His voice out of a crowd. The Bible teaches that Christ-followers can distinguish Jesus' voice among the others.

Read John 10:27-28.

What role do the Scriptures play in a Christ-follower's ability to recognize Jesus's voice/teachings?

Practically speaking, how is a believer able to differentiate Jesus' voice from others?

When crisis strikes, it's important for God's people to understand God's promises. We come to know God's character, understand His ways, and learn to apply His promises to our lives through spending regular time in God's Word. Jesus will never act contrary to the principles taught in His Word. If something doesn't align with the teachings of Scripture, we can know with confidence that it's incorrect. Obeying God's Word and spending time getting to know God through the study of the Scriptures doesn't exempt us from trouble, but it prepares us for the trouble that inevitably comes.

What spiritual practices do you currently engage in? Are there new habits you need to embrace? If so, what are they?

TAKE HEART

Read John 16:33.

Jesus warned that we will have trouble in this world,
so why are we often surprised when trouble comes?

Why is relying on Jesus' promises rather than
our own resources a game-changer?

Jesus acknowledged His followers would have trouble in this world, but He instructed us to "take heart" during those troubles because He has "overcome the world." Interestingly, the words "take heart" could also translated as "take courage." While we generally think of courage as an emotion or attribute that you either have or don't, Jesus is saying that's not the case. In fact, Jesus promises that we can live courageously even when we're scared to death and He commands us to take our courage directly from His hand—as much as we need. We live courageously by acknowledging His presence, remembering His promises and walking forward in His power.

Jesus said in the face of trouble we should, "take heart" or "take courage." On a day-to-day basis, what will that look like for you?

LIMITLESS COURAGE

To access the courage Jesus' provides, we have to take action; it's a choice we must make. Losing courage, on the other hand, happens on its own, when you're not paying attention.

Your heart will get lost if you let it. King David said the same thing in Psalm 27:13-14:

I would have lost heart, unless I had believed
That I would see the goodness of the LORD
In the land of the living.
Wait on the LORD;
Be of good courage,
And He shall strengthen your heart:
Wait, I say, on the LORD!
PSALM 27:13-14

According to David, what is the key to not losing heart?

Why is it so difficult for most people to "wait on the LORD"?
How do you respond when you are forced to wait?

What role does our faith have when it comes to waiting?

Belief is the antidote to losing heart. It puts the lens of faith in front of our eyes and gives us access to limitless courage. As we wait on the Lord, our hearts are strengthened and we see can what was seemingly impossible before. Regardless of what's weighing you down—whether it's a fight you had with your spouse this morning, a big assignment at work that is stressing you out, worry and depression, or a strained relationship—you have the Spirit-empowered ability to wait on the Lord and call on His name to receive a fresh infusion of power.

Based on this lesson, how will you prepare for the trials
you will inevitably face? List one takeaway.

End your time together praying that God will help you to take
courage. Use Psalm 27:13-14 as a guide for your prayer.

S.O.A.P.

John 3:19-21

*As you spend time in this week's Scripture readings pay special attention
to what God's Word has to say about light and darkness.*

SCRIPTURE

OBSERVATION

APPLICATION

PRAYER

S.O.A.P.

Matthew 5:14-16

SCRIPTURE

OBSERVATION

APPLICATION

PRAYER

S.O.A.P.

Ephesians 5:6-11

SCRIPTURE

OBSERVATION

APPLICATION

PRAYER

S.O.A.P.

Colossians 1:12-14

SCRIPTURE

OBSERVATION

APPLICATION

PRAYER

S.O.A.P.

1 John 2:9-11

SCRIPTURE

OBSERVATION

APPLICATION

PRAYER

———

Faith is the telescope that allows us to see the spiritual realities at play all around us.

———

WEEK 2
THE INVISIBLE WORLD

START

Welcome to Session 2.

In session 1, we looked at what it means for Jesus to "Turn off the Dark." In this week's session, we are going to discuss the invisible world—the unseen spiritual realities playing out all around us. If we are going to be people filled with faith, we need to be able to see beyond what we can see with our naked eye.

How would you describe the concept of "faith" to a non-believing friend?

What do you think it means to look at things through the lens of faith?

At any given moment, there's always more going on than what we can see with the naked eye. If you've ever spent anytime stargazing, you know this is true. On a cloudless, dark night, when you are far from civilization, it's possible to see as many as five thousand stars. But on a cloudy night you might not see hardly any. That doesn't mean they aren't there—there are always stars in the sky—you just can't always see them. So it is spiritually. You must not rely on the naked eye. Faith is the telescope that allows us to see the spiritual realities at play all around us.

Pray and ask God to use our time together. After praying, watch the video teaching.

WATCH

Video sessions available at Lifeway.com/Lion or with a subscription to SmallGroup.com

DISCUSS

1. In this week's video teaching, Levi tells a story about watching meteor showers with his family but it was a cloudy night that prevented them from seeing the magnitude of the light show. Why is this a helpful metaphor for our spiritual life?

2. Levi describes the following statement as the beating heart of this study, "We only see part of what is going on." In what ways have you found this statement to be true? How does hindsight tend to make this clearer?

3. In this season of life, how would you describe your faith? Are there areas where you are struggling? If so, what are they?

4. What does it mean to look at your circumstances through the telescope of faith? How does faith shift your perspective?

5. Levi discussed the fact that a lion's eye is more sophisticated than a human eye at discerning light, giving them a bigger view of the world than human beings. In what specific areas do you need to put on the lens of faith to see life "through the eyes of a lion"?

6. What spiritual practices are most helpful in building your faith? What steps are you taking to make them a part of your daily life?

Close your discussion with prayer. Remind those in your group to complete the personal studies and Bible reading over the next week.

PERSONAL STUDY 1
FIX YOUR GAZE

Every moment of every day, you are in an invisible battle that rages on. As real as the ancient ones you read about in history class and as current as the clips shown on the evening news. This is the war: every moment of every day, we must make the all-important choice of whether we will rely on the naked eye. Will we trust what we can see is there or believe what God says is there? This decision confronts us all the time. The apostle Paul taught about this battle in one of his letters:

We do not look at the things which are seen, but at the things which are not seen. For the things which are seen are temporary, but the things which are not seen are eternal.
2 CORINTHIANS 4:18

What does Paul tell us to fix our gaze on? What does it mean to look on things "which are not seen"?

Why does Paul instruct his readers not to pay less attention to their present troubles (what he calls "the things which are seen")?

Based on the passage above, why is it important to be mindful that there is more going on than what we can see with the naked eye?

On any given day, we have a choice about whether or not we are going to believe what our naked eye can see or believe what God says is really there. Most of the time, we shuffle along oblivious to what is actually happening. We drink our lattes and double-click our friends' pictures on Instagram, never giving thought to what is taking place in the spiritual realm. But when faced with overwhelming circumstances, we must be convinced that there is more to our reality than what we can see.

HIDDEN IN PLAIN SIGHT

Read 2 Kings 6:8-17.

Gehazi was a servant of the prophet Elisha. A bounty had been placed on Elisha's head and when Gehazi went outside early one morning he realized they were surrounded by enemies. Understandably, Gehazi was alarmed and warned Elisha, but Elisha was unfazed. In fact, Elisha told Gehazi they had their opponent outnumbered. But Elisha's words didn't align with what Gehazi had seen with his own eyes and he was unconvinced. So Elisha prayed, "LORD, I pray, open his eyes that he may see" (6:17). God answered Elisha's prayer, and when Gehazi looked again he could see they outnumbered their enemies.

When God opened Gehazi's eyes, the enemy was still present. His circumstance hadn't changed, but he was no longer afraid. What had changed?

Why is it important for us to understand that just because we can't see God working doesn't mean that He isn't?

Think for a moment about your most pressing concern. How might your fears decrease if you looked at your circumstances through the lens of faith?

In our prayer life, it's not uncommon for us to ask God to bless us or change our circumstances. Certainly, the Bible gives us permission and even encourages us to pray about everything. But if we're honest, we probably spend less time than we should praying for God to mature our faith and transform us. Throughout the Bible God's people often prayed for spiritual development and maturity. We just saw how Elisha prayed that God would open Gehazi's eyes to understand the spiritual reality around him. Likewise, in the opening lines of Paul's Letters, he habitually prayed for the spiritual lives of the people he was writing to (Rom 1:8-9; 1 Cor. 1:4-5; Col. 1:3-4). And in Luke 17:5 the disciples asked of Jesus, "Lord, increase our faith."

Think for a moment about your prayer life. How often do you ask
God to enhance your spiritual life and increase your faith?

_____

Seldom   Sometimes   Frequently

Do you believe that it's God will for you to be a person of great faith? Why
or why not? What prevents you from asking God to increase your faith?

When you pray for those close to you, how often do you ask God to
increase their faith? Who do you know who needs prayer in this area?

THE TELESCOPE OF FAITH

Nothing makes us question our faith more than when we are in the middle of a disaster
and can't see the way out. But it's during times of testing when we decide what we really
believe about God. It's easy to say we trust God when everyone is healthy, and there is
money in the bank. But when we don't understand what God is doing and can't sense His
presence, our faith is tested. Paul found himself in more than his fair share of tight spots.
He wrote:

> For we do not want you to be ignorant, brethren, of our trouble which came
> to us in Asia: that we were burdened beyond measure, above strength, so
> that we despaired even of life. Yes, we had the sentence of death in ourselves,
> that we should not trust in ourselves but in God who raises the dead.
>
> 2 CORINTHIANS 1:8-9

Notice Paul said they were "burdened beyond measure." How does a dire situation position a believer to view their struggle through a lens of faith?

According to the verses, what did Paul's hardships teach him?

When have you ever experienced a situation that forced you to rely on God rather than yourself? If so, what did you learn?

It feels miserable when we are confronted with a series of events that are beyond our control, but oftentimes it's the only way we truly learn to trust God rather than ourselves. When we are in a difficult situation and we can't see the way out, we have no choice but to exclusively trust God. It's in those times when we come to know and experience God in ways we never have before.

End your time today praying for God to increase your faith.

PERSONAL STUDY 2
SATAN'S WEAPONS:
BREAD AND CIRCUSES

A lion's eyes are sophisticated at discerning light. They can see things you and me can't see with our naked eye. Through the eyes of a lion is a metaphor to describe the life of faith because through a "lion's lens," we have the ability to see an unseen reality all around us.

However, if we want to be people of faith who see our circumstances through the eyes of a lion, buckle up because Satan wants nothing more than to see you back down. Satan would love for you to think that when he comes to mess with you he'll show up in a red suit with a pitchfork but that would be far too obvious. He often resorts to an approach that is much more sly, and far more dangerous, something called "panem circenses" it's Latin for "bread and circuses," and it's part of a quote from a Roman writer named Juvenal around 100 AD:

> For the People who once upon a time handed out military
> command, high civil office, legions—everything, now restrains itself
> and anxiously hopes for just two things: bread and circuses.
> JUVENAL SATIRE, 10.81

Juvenal was describing the way the people of the Roman Empire had been tricked to giving up their freedom. All it had taken them to forfeit their freedom was bread and circuses, in other words—food and entertainment took their focus off the greater issues and in the process they lost their freedom because they were distracted. In the same way, Satan doesn't want us to experience the freedom that Christ died to give us. He knows that if he can distract us from Jesus he can destroy us.

Read 2 Corinthians 11:3.

Why is distraction an effective tool to use against believers?

List three distractions that could be harmful to your relationship with Christ.

1.

2.

3.

How does distraction lead us to take our eyes off Jesus?

THE DEVIL DEALS IN DISTRACTION

The devil wants you to forfeit what Christ died for you to have, and one of his most effective tools is distraction. Destruction by distraction is difficult to detect when it's happening, because it doesn't always involve bad things but good things that take the place of the most important things. But the things that appear good to us are not always good for us. The apostle Peter warned about losing our focus:

> *Be sober, be vigilant; because your adversary the devil walks about like a roaring lion, seeking whom he may devour. Resist him, steadfast in the faith, knowing that the same sufferings are experienced by your brotherhood in the world.*
>
> 1 PETER 5:8-9.

What reason did Peter give for believers to stay focused?

Why is distraction so difficult to see in your own life?

What can you do to guard against spiritual distraction? Who is a friend that you can give permission to speak out against your distraction?

DON'T TAKE THE BAIT

The devil wants to steal your power and neutralize your impact. Don't fall for his tricks. His goal is to trick you with the trivial and get you to spend your life focused on the superficial, to keep you from your calling and deprive you of the life Jesus died to give you. His endgame is to play the fiddle while the life you were meant to live goes up in smoke.

On a scale of 1-10, how big of an issue is distraction for you?

What "good things" in your life are you tempted to make the "ultimate thing?"

What steps can you take to address and neutralize your distractions?

What are some better things you can use to refocus your life on Jesus?

Don't mistake what I'm saying. Football, good meals, cycling, travel, Twitter, and fashion—these are all good gifts from God, given to us for our enjoyment. I'm convinced that He takes pleasure when we enjoy our lives (Eccl. 9:7-8). He smiles when we eat and laugh, run and play. But these things, in and of themselves, aren't enough. We were never supposed to live our lives purely on the physical playing field. We were created for more.

WE DON'T BELONG HERE

In our day-to-day life, we sometimes get so caught up in the rhythm and fast pace that we forget there's more to our existence than the life we are living. In fact, God made us for eternity. In the apostle Paul's letter to the church at Philippi, he issued a warning to those he called enemies of the cross and reminded believers that we are not to focus only on earthly things. Paul wrote:

> *They are headed for destruction. Their god is their appetite, they brag about shameful things, and they think only about this life here on earth. But we are citizens of heaven, where the Lord Jesus Christ lives. And we are eagerly waiting for him to return as our Savior.*
> PHILIPPIANS 3:19-20, NLT

In the above passage, what suggests that the people (the enemies of the cross) had been led astray by distraction?

Why is it counterproductive for Christians to focus exclusively on the "here and now?"

How do Paul's words above of Philippians support the concept of the "invisible world" we have studied this week?

Paul told believers at the church in Philippi that they were citizens of heaven (3:20). As a Christian, the same is true for you. You live here, but heaven is your home. If you have put your faith in Christ, this world is no longer your home. You are just passing through.

End your time today praying that God will reveal unhealthy distractions in your life.

S.O.A.P.

2 Corinthians 10:3-5

In this week's lesson we spend time studying the invisible world and what it means to stay alert. As you spend time in this week's Scripture readings pay special attention to what God's Word has to say about this topic.

SCRIPTURE

OBSERVATION

APPLICATION

PRAYER

S.O.A.P.

Ephesians 6:10-18

SCRIPTURE

OBSERVATION

APPLICATION

PRAYER

S.O.A.P.

Mark 13:32-37

SCRIPTURE

OBSERVATION

APPLICATION

PRAYER

S.O.A.P.

Hebrews 13:14-16

SCRIPTURE

OBSERVATION

APPLICATION

PRAYER

S.O.A.P.

John 14:1-3

SCRIPTURE

OBSERVATION

APPLICATION

PRAYER

——

Hope is the confident expectation that
God will do what He promised.

——

WEEK 3

HURTING WITH HOPE

START

Welcome to Session 3.

In week 2, we discussed the invisible world and what it looks like to have the eyes of a lion even when we can't see everything that is going on. This week, we'll be studying what it means to hurt with hope. Grief has the ability to cloud our vision, but we can learn to walk by faith in the midst of suffering.

What are some of the most common ways people express grief?

In our culture, do you think people do a good job comforting those who are hurting? Why or why not?

When you're hurting, what are the most helpful things your friends and family can do to support you?

All of us experience times of grief and suffering. Believing in Jesus doesn't exempt us from emotional hardship, and being a Christian doesn't mean we won't shed tears during our time on earth. However, it does mean that when we do hurt, we do so with the knowledge that our best days are ahead of us and a time is coming when all sadness will come to an end.

Pray and ask God to use our time together.
After praying, watch the video teaching.

WATCH

Use this section to take notes as you watch video session 3.

DISCUSS

1. In the video, Levi said "God doesn't expect us to be robots in our faith. When we get saved our emotions don't come unplugged." Why do you think some Christians wrongly believe they shouldn't show emotion? Do you think this idea comes from our culture or our faith?

2. Grieving people often apologize for crying in front of other people. Why do you think people feel the need to apologize when they show emotion? Why is the urge to apologize unhealthy?

3. Think about times you have experienced suffering or grief. How did those times grow or shape your faith?

4. Levi said, "God is honored by the worship you give Him when you understand Him the least." Why is it a sign of spiritual maturity if we can worship God even when we don't understand our circumstances?

5. What does it means to "hurt with hope"?

6. In times of suffering, what difference has your faith made? How would the experience be different if you had no faith?

Close your discussion with prayer. Remind those in your group to complete the personal studies and Bible reading over the next week.

PERSONAL STUDY 1

HURTING WITH HOPE

Hope is a word that gets thrown around a lot in our vocabulary. It's not uncommon to hear someone say, "I hope things work out." Or, "I hope it doesn't rain on Saturday." In this context, hope is passive and carries no more punch than wishful thinking. But biblical hope is different than secular hope. Biblical hope means we can have confidence in the future based on God's promises found in the Scriptures.[1] (Eerdmans, p. 605). Biblical hope carries a connotation of confident expectation based on the fact that the God of the Bible is faithful to keep His Word. The writer of Hebrews said:

This hope we have as an anchor of the soul, both sure and
steadfast, and which enters the Presence behind the veil.

HEBREWS 6:19

HOPE IS AN ANCHOR

How did the writer of Hebrews describe hope? What
about this description most resonates with you?

What is the purpose of an anchor? How can hope serve
as an anchor in the middle of a personal storm?

What are your biggest obstacles to remaining hopeful? What fuels your hope?

The symbol of the anchor is powerful because of what it stands for: hope. When the author of Hebrews speaks of "this hope we have as an anchor of the soul" it's life-changing. A boat that is anchored can be battered, but it won't be moved. Because of Jesus, we have hope. And because of hope, even in the worst storms of life, we have an anchor for our souls.

In what areas do you need a renewed sense of hope?

What specific Scriptures speak to your current situation?
How might you rely on these Scriptures as an anchor?

Hope is a powerful thing. The most important battle is the one you fight within, in your mind and heart, to not give up. At its most basic level, to have hope is to believe that something good is going to happen. That help is on the way. That it's not over yet, and no matter how dark it seems, there's going to be light at the end of the tunnel. Hope is a confident expectation that God will do what He has promised. When you have hope, gale-force winds can blow and waves can smash into the hull of your life, but you are buoyed by the belief that the best is yet to come. Brighter days are ahead. Hope quietly tells your heart that all is not lost, even as storms rage because our hope takes us directly to God. Look again at Hebrews:

This hope ... enters the Presence behind the veil,
where the forerunner has entered for us.
HEBREWS 6:19-20

According to the writer of Hebrews, where does hope lead us?

The "veil" the writer of Hebrews referred to is the curtain in the temple that separated the outer area of the temple from the most holy place where the high priest experienced the presence of God. When Jesus rose from the dead and ascended to heaven, He entered into God's throne room blazing a trail for us. He took our anchor and connected it to the altar there behind the veil.

HOPE IS A PERSON

Jesus entered the throne room of heaven as a "forerunner" so we could follow in His footsteps. The Greek word translated "forerunner" was used to describe a pilot boat that would go ahead of a large vessel in a harbor that was sketchy to navigate. This large ship would give their anchor to the pilot boat and he would take the anchor through the harbor safely to shore. In the same way, Jesus paved the way to heaven bringing our anchor behind the veil where it is permanently fixed. Now, we are slowly but surely every day of our lives being winched in, inch by inch, to the distant shores of our true homeland, where true hope is found. The thing about anchors is that to be effective, they must be attached to something, they never come in Bluetooth and they don't work with Wi-Fi. There is no place more secure to anchor our hope than in Jesus.

If our ultimate hope is found in Jesus, why do we regularly place our hope in other things?

Where are some places you are tempted to place your hope?

What changes do you need to make to anchor your hope in Jesus?

If we aren't careful, it's easy to unintentionally put our hope in things that don't have the capability to deliver. Our family and friends, good health, and material resources are all blessings we should enjoy, but they shouldn't be the source of our ultimate hope. We must choose to hope in God.

HOPE IS A DECISION

In the passage that follows, Peter instructs believers on where they should place their hope:

Through Him believe in God, who raised Him from the dead and gave Him glory, so that your faith and hope are in God.
1 PETER 1:21

Where does Peter instruct us to place our hope?

According to 1 Peter 1:21, why do we have good reason to place our hope in God?

What difference would it make if you lived with an expectant hope regarding your current circumstances?

Peter makes it clear that because God raised Christ from the dead, we have every reason to place our faith and hope in the power of God. But living with hope is a choice we make daily. It's not a one and done decision. Each morning, we decide to focus on our circumstances or fix our gaze on Jesus and the promises God has revealed to us in the Scriptures. Of course, from time to time we all get down and it's easy to shift our gaze and lose hope. But when we do, we can quickly realign our thoughts and shift our focus back to the truth that Jesus is for us and with us in our troubles.

End your time today asking God to fill you with hope in Christ and the promises of God.

PERSONAL STUDY 2
HURTING WITH HOPE
STILL HURTS

And now, dear brothers and sisters, we want you to know
what will happen to the believers who have died so you
will not grieve like people who have no hope.
1 THESSALONIANS 4:13, NLT

If you've been a Christian for any length of time and lost a loved one, there's a good chance you're familiar with this passage. And it's true, because of our hope in Christ, believers grieve differently than those without hope. The promises of God and our future in heaven have a direct impact on the way we anticipate the future. But here's something you need to know: hurting with hope still hurts. The sting of death might have been removed, but it still stings. It hurts even when you know your loved one is in heaven. No, we might not grieve as those who have no hope, but that doesn't mean we won't be sad.

Have you ever experienced a time when you felt like you should hide your grief? If so, what caused you to feel that way?

Who are you most likely to reach out to when you are grieving? What makes this person/people a source of comfort?

We do a disservice anytime we try to rush people through the process of grief, as though it were spiritual to put a happy face on a horrible thing. Masking pain doesn't heal it any faster; it actually slows it down and stunts your rehabilitation. Sadness is an entirely appropriate emotion and a feeling Jesus demonstrated in the Bible.

JESUS SHARES OUR SORROW

Even if we have hope, it doesn't mean we're happy about our sorrow. But God isn't happy about sorrow either. In fact, He's furious. Not about our hope, but that we would need it. That's why He warned Adam and Eve in the garden to avoid the forbidden fruit (Gen. 2:17). God knew that sin would trigger death. He never intended for us to struggle in the surf, with wave after wave of sadness crashing upon us. But in His goodness, He doesn't leave us alone in our sorrow. When Jesus' friends were grieving He went to them and comforted them.

Read John 11:1-36.

What stands out to you about this passage? In John 11, we see that Jesus sought out Lazarus' sisters—Mary and Martha. Why is it important to be present with those who are grieving?

Glance back at verse 35. Jesus already knew that He was going to raise Lazarus from the dead, so why do you think He wept?

JESUS WEPT

We see how Jesus really feels about grief and death in John 11. Jesus wept at Lazarus's death. He didn't attempt to hide His emotion or disguise His sadness. He didn't say, "It's OK! Lazarus has gone to a better place, everybody. He's probably playing football in my Father's house." No, Jesus cried. He cried because He hates death more than we do. He cried because Mary and Martha were suffering. And He cried because the world isn't yet how it should be.

How should Jesus' tears inform your views about grieving?

**Does the image of Jesus weeping bring you comfort
or make you uncomfortable? Explain**

The thought of Jesus weeping is shocking, but even more shocking is what came next. The Bible says that Jesus groaned in His spirit (v. 33). This was no ordinary sigh. The Greek word used here means "to bellow with rage."[2] It's a word that's so strong it's normally used to describe the angry snorting of an agitated horse. So much for gentle Jesus, meek and mild. He was fuming. Absolutely outraged. Mad at death. Mad at the grave, at sin, at the devil. But He wasn't just angry—He was angry enough to do something about it.

Read John 11:37-41. Why is it appropriate for us to hate death?

**Do you ever think that because God allows death and suffering
He must be OK with it? How would it change things if you
were mindful that God hates suffering more than anyone?**

JESUS TRIUMPHED OVER DEATH

To be sure, Jesus raising Lazarus from the dead was an impressive act of power but that wasn't Jesus' endgame. Remember, Lazarus would have to die all over again. Any physical miracle is just a delaying of the inevitable. Jesus was always focused on the spiritual miracle because that would last forever. So what did Jesus do after raising Lazarus from the dead? He went on to defeat death in the most unlikely way ever—by dying.

*Inasmuch then as the children have partaken of flesh and blood, He
Himself likewise shared in the same, that through death He might destroy
him who had the power of death, that is, the devil, and release those
who through fear of death were all their lifetime subject to bondage.*
HEBREWS 2:14-15

How did Jesus' death lead to victory over death?

Jesus didn't simply die. Anyone can do that. Wait long enough, and it will happen to you. Jesus didn't just die—He rose from the dead. His soul reentered His decaying body, and He got up! Unbelievably, He offers this same casket-exploding power to anyone who believes. This is the gospel—Jesus died to destroy death and release those who believe in Him from the fear and power of death. Christians grieve with hope because in the end, they have a Savior who will wipe every tear from their eyes (Rev. 21:4).

How does understanding that Jesus triumphed over death change the way you live in the here and now?

Hurting with hope doesn't mean we don't get sad, but hope changes things. How does hope influence your suffering and sorrows?

End your time today in prayer praising Christ for triumphing over death.

1. David Noel Freedman, *Eerdmans Dictionary of the Bible,* Grand Rapids: Wm.B. Eerdsmans, 2000.
2. Tim Keller, *The Grieving Sisters,* Encounters With Jesus3, Kindle ed. (New York: Penguin, 2013) loc 189-91;
   A.T. Robertson, *Word Pictures in the New Testament* (Nashville: Broadman, 1933). John 11:33.

S.O.A.P.

Romans 5:1-5

This week we studied what it means to hurt with hope. As you spend time in this week's Scripture readings pay special attention to what God's Word has to say about Hope.

SCRIPTURE

OBSERVATION

APPLICATION

PRAYER

S.O.A.P.

Romans 12:9-14

SCRIPTURE

OBSERVATION

APPLICATION

PRAYER

S.O.A.P.

1 Corinthians 13:8-13

SCRIPTURE

OBSERVATION

APPLICATION

PRAYER

S.O.A.P.

2 Peter 3:13-16

SCRIPTURE

OBSERVATION

APPLICATION

PRAYER

S.O.A.P.

Psalm 42:1-5

SCRIPTURE

OBSERVATION

APPLICATION

PRAYER

———

Death isn't the end of the story. We must fight to remember that the grave doesn't get the last word.

———

WEEK 4
THE HOPE OF HEAVEN

START

Welcome to Session 4.

Last session, we studied what it means to hurt with hope. In this week's lesson we'll take a close look at what believers have to look forward to in the hope of heaven. We'll spend time learning what Paul has to say about life in this world compared to the life to come. We'll learn that death is not the end of our story.

What comes to mind when you think about heaven?

Do you think movies and TV shows have done an accurate job depicting heaven? Why or why not?

Why is it so difficult for people to talk about the reality of death?

When someone dies, it's not uncommon for a well-meaning person to say, "He's in a better place." But for Christians, we don't have to live with such a vague notion of heaven because the Bible isn't silent about the issue. This session will focus on the hope of heaven.

Pray and ask God to use our time together.
After praying, watch the video teaching.

WATCH

Video sessions available at Lifeway.com/Lion or with a subscription to SmallGroup.com

DISCUSS

After viewing the video, discuss the following questions with your group.

1. In the video, Levi mentioned, "Ignoring death doesn't make it go away" and that the only thing certain in this life is it's going to end, so to have no plan isn't a wise strategy. Why do you think so many people ignore death instead of plan for it?

2. Where do you imagine most people form their views about heaven—from culture or from the Bible? What are some false views people hold about heaven?

3. Jesus said, "I am the way, the truth, and the life. No one comes to the Father except through Me" (John 14:6). What does this passage teach about how we get to heaven? How is this teaching different from what many people believe about heaven?

4. Why is it important to have a biblical view of heaven?

5. How does knowledge about heaven make the death of a loved one or a terminal diagnosis feel less overwhelming? When has this hope been a comfort you? Share if you feel comfortable.

6. Levi said, "Death isn't leaving home; it's going home." What did he mean by that? Do you see heaven this way? Why or why not?

Close your discussion with prayer. Remind those in your group to complete the personal studies and Bible reading over the next week.

PERSONAL STUDY 1
A TEMPORARY DWELLING

Several months after Lenya went to heaven, we found a video of her we'd never seen. Lenya was wearing a Snow White dress, wildly spinning and whirling around the room. Finally, out of juice, Lenya laid on the ground and said dramatically, "I die." Believe it or not, this is common behavior for a little girl wearing a Snow White dress. In the movie, the Disney princess eats a poisoned apple that makes her fall into a deep sleep that only true love can wake. As we watched the video, tears forming in our eyes, we assumed this is what Lenya had in mind. After lying perfectly still for a few moments, she suddenly stood and declared, "And get back up … with Jesus … in heaven! The video was filmed five days before Lenya did just that.

Read 2 Corinthians 5:1-8.

**What metaphor did Paul use to describe our bodies here on earth?
Name a few reasons why this is an appropriate comparison.**

**In verse 4, Paul says we "groan while we are in this tent."
What are common reasons for our groaning?**

**Glance back at verse 7. How does faith shape
the way we experience our lives?**

A PERMANENT DWELLING

After Lenya went to heaven, digging into 2 Corinthians 5 gave me strength and peace in ways I will never be able to articulate. Paul basically says that this life is a camping trip. Instead of canvas and poles, we are all camping in tents made flesh and blood. But what goes up must come down. The more you use a tent, the more trashed it gets. Paul knew this better than anyone—he was a tentmaker. Paul didn't just make new tents; he patched up old ones. Eventually, though, a tent is irreparable and can't be used anymore. That is death.

Think for a moment about the struggles of living in a body that is subject to age and illness. In what ways will our new eternal dwelling be an upgrade?

When has your body caused you pain? Name a few of the ways that shedding this temporary body will be a relief to you.

Glance back at 2 Corinthians 5:5. What does Paul identify as the down payment on our new dwelling?

No camping trip lasts forever. We all must break camp sooner or later. But, Paul insists, when that happens, all is not lost. When this tent dissolves, we have a house in heaven. In the Roman empire, tents were often used as temporary dwellings while houses were being constructed. When the home was finally ready, you left the tent and went back to your home. The departure was an upgrade. For us, stepping away from our earthly tents and into the house Jesus has prepared for us is also an upgrade (John 14:3).

AT HOME WITH THE LORD

Yes, we are fully confident, and we would rather be away from these earthly bodies, for then we will be at home with the Lord.
2 CORINTHIANS 5:8 (NLT)

Paul says in the above text we "would prefer to be away from the body and at home with the Lord." For the Christian, why is Jesus our ultimate home?

As agonizing and painful as it can be, death is the ultimate upgrade for the believer: moving from the tent into the home Jesus has been preparing for you. When your earthly tent finally breaks down, you will open your eyes in the glory and majesty of heaven. Death is not the end of the road; it's just a bend in the road. Believers take their last breath here on earth and the next breath in the presence of God in heaven. In the weeks and months following Lenya's death, I reminded myself of these truths. When I looked at the situation through the telescope of faith, my spine filled with steel and fear was replaced with faith.

Read John 5:28-29.

What stands out most to you about Jesus' words in this passage?

How do Jesus' words change or challenge your view about death?

How do these passages add insight to Paul's words in 1 Corinthians 15:55 "O Death, where is your sting?"

DEATH ISN'T THE END OF THE STORY

We must fight to remember that the grave doesn't get the last word. The body that was taken from us will be returned in our resurrection. The very word "cemetery" itself comes from the Latin word "dormitory" and means "sleeping place." One day Jesus will give a wake-up call to the bodies in the dorms, and they will rise. The resurrection of our bodies is not immediate, though; there is an interval. From the moment you die until the moment Jesus returns, you will be in heaven but not back in your resurrection body (John 14:3-4; 1 Thess. 4:13-18).

We place a lot of emphasis on our physical bodies and it's true we should take care of them. But how do these biblical truths about our physical bodies put things in perspective?

Would you say most people put greater focus on their physical bodies or their spiritual life? Explain why you feel the way you do.

As you read this session, you might be wondering what our bodies will be like when we get to heaven, prior to the time when our bodies are resurrected from the grave. There is nothing I wish I knew more than this. Some people think that God grants physical properties to souls upon entry to paradise. Others theorize that temporary bodies are prepared. We really don't know. There are at least three bodies in heaven, though: Elijah, Enoch, and Jesus all went there without leaving physical bodies behind, so we know it is a location suitable for living with a body (Gen. 5:24; 2 Kings 2:11; Luke 24:51). However the details shake out, there's no way people in heaven are distressed to be away from the bodies they left on earth. The resurrection of our bodies is not because of necessity but because of desire. It will happen because God has the power, ability, and desire to make it happen.

End your time today thanking Jesus for conquering death.

PERSONAL STUDY 2
HEAVEN IS A PLACE

There's nothing I can't stand more than the lame heaven myths that have been endlessly perpetuated by the devil to keep us from looking forward to it. People floating on clouds, everything looking translucent, Gregorian chants playing endlessly on the sounds system, and—of course—chubby, naked baby angels flitting around. For the record, I have read the entire Bible, and I haven't found a single mention of any of these things. But the Bible isn't silent on the issue.

Read Luke 23:32-43.

What stands out to you about this passage?

As Jesus hung on the cross, He was surrounded by a criminal on each side. How did these two men face their death differently?

TWO RESPONSES TO JESUS

Unlike the criminal who was mocking Jesus, the other understood that Jesus was the Son of God and that He was being unjustly punished (23:41). One man asked Jesus to remember him when he came into His kingdom (23:42). One mocked the Son of God and the other asked for eternal life and Jesus granted it. The two men used their last hours on earth very differently. At the end of our time on earth, the most important thing will be how we responded to Jesus.

> One of the criminals was granted eternal life just minutes
> or hours before his death. But why is it wise to address
> the issue of eternal life sooner rather than later?

> Glance back at verse 43. What word did Jesus use to describe
> heaven? What images does that create in your mind?

It's notable that Jesus said, "Assuredly, I say to you, today you will be with Me in Paradise" (v. 43). Paradise provokes a variety of thoughts and images and they are all outrageously good. The Bible also makes is clear that heaven is a real place. Like New York or Paris, heaven is a location. Untainted by sin and disease, and unspoiled by evil, it's a physical place like earth, but much better. Heaven is full of fulfillment and happiness—all infused and energized by the presence of God and pulsating with holy wonder.

> What do you anticipate most about heaven?

A PRAYER OF FAITH

Heaven is a real place that Christ-followers can look forward to with hope-filled expectation. But the reality is, only those who have trusted Christ as their Savior will go there (John 14:6; Acts 4:12). This is what God wants for you: Forgiveness. A relationship with you. Heaven. Jesus left heaven and came to earth so we could go to heaven when we leave earth. The Bible promises that if you believe in your heart that Jesus is Lord, and confess with your mouth that He rose from the dead, you will be saved. You can pray something as simple as this:

> *God, I believe that I am a sinner. I'm broken, and I can't fix myself.*
> *I believe that Jesus is your Son and that He died on the cross in my place.*
> *I believe that He rose from the dead. I turn from my sins and to you.*
> *Please forgive me and help my follow you. In Jesus' name I pray, amen.*

A simple childlike faith in Jesus is the power to change your heart and save your soul forever.

Do you have assurance that when your time on earth is over you will spend eternity with God? If not, what obstacles stand in your way?

How does the assurance of your salvation impact your thoughts about death?

This life is not all there is. When we leave this world, we get to go home. And the way we live here has a direct impact on what we experience when we arrive there. Before we know it, we will be standing before God to receive our reward. This tent is dissolving. It's fragile, vulnerable, and temporary, and it will soon come down. We have no way of knowing when it will end.

TREASURE IN HEAVEN

How does the hope of heaven influence how you live?

Getting to heaven has nothing to do with our righteous works. Our entrance fee is paid fully by Jesus and His perfect sacrifice (Eph. 2:8-9, 1 John 2:2). But Scripture is clear that although our salvation is not based on our works—our treasure in heaven is connected to our lives on earth (Matt. 6:4, 16:27; 1 Cor. 3:13-15; 2 Cor. 5:10; 1 Tim. 6:17-19).

Although good works can't obtain God's salvation, how we spend our time on earth influences our heavenly reward. With that in mind, how do you think God is calling you to spend your time?

If you knew you had limited time left, what would you be sure to do?

The devil will do anything he can do to keep you from sensing the urgency that will mark your life if you wake up each day knowing it could be your last. He won't try to talk you out of doing the things you intended to; he'll simply tell you to put it off. One of his biggest lies is, "You can do it tomorrow." He knows what you need to know—there might not be a tomorrow. A thousand years from now, we won't be able to change what we did in our lifetimes, but if we do it right, we will be enjoying the fruits of it.

What are you currently putting off because "there's always tomorrow"?

End your time today by praying the words written by Moses in Psalm 90.

So teach us to number our days,
That we may gain a heart of wisdom.
Return, O LORD!
How long?
And have compassion on Your servants.
Oh, satisfy us early with Your mercy,
That we may rejoice and be glad all our days!
Make us glad according to the days in which You have afflicted us,
The years in which we have seen evil.
Let Your work appear to Your servants,
And Your glory to their children.
And let the beauty of the LORD our God be upon us,
And establish the work of our hands for us;
Yes, establish the work of our hands.

PSALM 90:12-17

S.O.A.P.

Romans 10:6-10

This week we spent time studying the hope of heaven. As you spend time in this week's Scripture readings pay special attention to what God's Word has to say about this topic.

SCRIPTURE

OBSERVATION

APPLICATION

PRAYER

S.O.A.P.

Matthew 6:19-21

SCRIPTURE

OBSERVATION

APPLICATION

PRAYER

S.O.A.P.

Philippians 3:20-21

SCRIPTURE

OBSERVATION

APPLICATION

PRAYER

S.O.A.P.

1 Corinthians 15:35-40

SCRIPTURE

OBSERVATION

APPLICATION

PRAYER

S.O.A.P.

Psalm 19:1-6

SCRIPTURE

OBSERVATION

APPLICATION

PRAYER

———

When our spiritual batteries are running low, all we have to do is wait on the Lord and ask Him for strength. God promises that help will flow in response to such a request.

———

CUE THE EAGLE

START

Welcome to Session 5.

Last week, we took an in-depth look at the hope of heaven. This week we'll discuss what it looks like to be prepared for times of suffering. We'll learn what it means to cue the eagle and we'll highlight practical ways we can spiritually prepare ourselves for whatever comes our way.

> **Share about a time when you were caught off guard. What happened and how did you respond? What did you learn?**

> **When is the last time you had to wait longer than you expected for something? How did you respond to the delay?**

Sometimes the things that we're hoping to happen take longer than anticipated or transpire in a way that lead to disappointment. During times of waiting, disappointment, or grief we're prone to become weary. In this week's session, we'll learn what it means to draw on God's strength rather than our own.

> *Pray and ask God to use our time together.*
> *After praying, watch the video teaching.*

WATCH

Video sessions available at Lifeway.com/Lion or with a subscription to SmallGroup.com

DISCUSS

---

1. If you knew a difficult season of life was on the horizon, what types of things would you like to have in place beforehand?

2. In this week's video, Levi said that it's wise to "Train for the trial you're not yet in." Spiritually speaking, what are some of the ways you can prepare for trials?

3. Levi discussed that "Saturday is the space between promise and fulfillment" and he used the example of the Good Friday and Christ's Resurrection on Sunday. Is there a specific area in your life that feels like "Saturday" to you? If so, what is it?

4. Why is it easy to lose heart when we are in a waiting pattern?

5. What role does your local church play in a time of hardship?

6. Why are seasons of suffering more intense when we feel like we're alone? What role do other people have in helping you through difficult situations? What role do you have when someone you know is suffering?

7. On a day-to-day basis, what does it look like for a believer to rely on God's strength rather than his/her own?

      Close your discussion with prayer. Remind those in your group to
      complete the personal studies and Bible reading over the next week.

PERSONAL STUDY 1
GET READY TO WAIT

As Americans, we live in a fast-paced culture and don't like to wait. We're accustomed to overnight shipping, high-speed internet, fast food, and instant access. When things don't go as quickly as planned, we suspect something has gone wrong. If a company can't meet our demand for speed, we take our business elsewhere. But the reality is, the Bible records a long history of God's people waiting on God to act. We will experience times of waiting too. There will also be times when things aren't going as quickly as we'd prefer. Consider the words of the apostle Peter:

> *But, beloved, do not forget this one thing, that with the Lord one day is as a thousand years, and a thousand years as one day.*
> 2 PETER 3:8

How do you respond to unexpected wait times?

How would you explain the concept of waiting to a child?

Why do you think God's timing is so different than ours?

THE SILENCE OF SATURDAY

If you want an example of an excruciating wait, look no further than the weekend of Christ's resurrection. Between Jesus' burial on Friday and His resurrection on Sunday, there was Saturday. Good Friday is famous and Easter Sunday is awesome, so we understandably think and talk about these two days most often. But that Saturday must have been a day of crushing disappointment. It was a time when promises had been made but were not yet fulfilled. The disciples were in a waiting pattern and they had no clue how long it might last. Jesus said He would come back. He said death wouldn't be the end of the story. But then there was silence. It seemed as though things hadn't gone as planned. That Saturday the disciples didn't know they were on the brink of the greatest event in world history. Saturday was filled with nothing but loss. Jesus' body laid dead, decaying, and cold. Scripture mentions little about Saturday—because nothing notable happened.

What types of things do you think were going through the disciples' minds the Saturday before the resurrection?

The silent Saturday before resurrection Sunday demonstrates the reality that just because we can't see God working doesn't mean He isn't. Why is that so important to remember during times of hardship?

For the disciples, Saturday lasted way too long. For some of them, the mood of Saturday continued into Sunday morning—even after Jesus had risen from the grave.

WE HAD HOPED ...

Read Luke 24:13-35.

Glance back at verses 21-24. Why do you think the two men had such a resigned attitude?

If you'd been in their situation how do you think you would've responded?

In verse 27, Jesus begins to interpret the Old Testament Scriptures in light of the Easter weekend events. Why do you think the men failed to make the connection?

How do we sometimes fail to connect our circumstances with God's will for our lives?

WHEN SATURDAY LINGERS

We too, are living in the spirit of an extended Saturday. We have a living Savior, so we have a living hope. God is like an elephant when it comes to His promises—He never forgets. Jesus will come back. We will get to see our Savior's face. What the enemy has destroyed will be restored. But not yet. It's still Saturday, and sometimes it seems as if Saturday will last forever.

Saturday is …

When a child knows he will meet his dad in heaven someday but right now can only look at pictures.

When a person with paralysis has the promise of a new body free of wheelchairs and numbness but still has to struggle through years on end in the body she's in.

When families celebrate birthday and holidays but feel the weight of the empty chair at the table.

Do any of these examples of "Saturday" resonate with you? If so, which one? If not, what does "Saturday" look like for you?

REASON TO HOPE

Let us hold fast the confession of our hope without wavering, for He who promised is faithful. And let us consider one another in order to stir up love and good works, not forsaking the assembling of ourselves together, as is the manner of some, but exhorting one another, and so much the more as you see the Day approaching.
HEBREWS 10:23-25

In seasons of waiting, we can rest assured God is faithful to keep His promises. But to make the time easier to bear, the Scriptures encourage us to gather together with God's people. God never intended for us to struggle alone. During seasons of struggle, the Church is one of the primary ways God shows His grace to us. As we follow Jesus, we do it together.

On a scale of 1-10, how active are you in biblical community?

If you aren't an active member of a local church, what steps can you take to get plugged in?

End your time today praying for those you know who are in a Saturday season.

PERSONAL STUDY 2
BAD DAYS AND GOOD COMPANY

All of us have bad days. In some seasons of life, our struggles and hardships are difficult to bear. No matter how thick your skin is, how may Bible verses you have memorized, or how high your pain threshold is, even the best men are men at best. Everyone has a breaking point. Just look at the lives of those we would consider the strongest characters in Scripture:

- King David was a man after God's own heart. For decades, he held on to God's promise that he would become king. But then he gave up and moved to Goliath's native country, where he worked for a Philistine king and fought the wrong battles (1 Sam. 27).
- Abraham, the father of faith, ran away from the promised land and lied about his wife being his sister to protect himself. Why? He was afraid (Genesis 20).
- The apostle Paul begged God three times to take away a painful trial that was too heavy for him to carry (2 Cor. 12:7-8).
- Elijah, the mightiest of the miracle-working prophets, had an emotional breakdown when a woman cussed him out. He ran away from home, hid under a tree, and wished for death (1 Kings 19:4).
- The prophet Jeremiah became so discouraged that he told God he was never going to preach again (Jer.20:9).
- John the Baptist is the man who Jesus once said was the best person ever to be born of a woman wondered whether Jesus was the Messiah he'd been waiting for (Luke 7:20).

My point here isn't to bash on the people in the Bible. My point is to show that we all struggle. These guys were giants of the faith and yet they all ran out of strength. And guess what? So will you. Especially when you are forced to face the endurance sport that is grief. Whether your grief is from the death of a marriage, the end of a friendship, or the loss of a position at work, there will be times, even as a believer, when you are pushed to your limits and beyond. I know, probably not the encouraging pep talk you came here to read. But the good news is, when God's people run low on our own strength, we have a source of power we can rely on.

CUE THE EAGLE

There's a scene somewhere in the nine hours of the Lord of the Rings films where Gandalf the Grey is about to be killed but is saved at the last minute when an enormous eagle swoops in and carries him away. Something similar happens in one of The Hobbit movies. A bunch of vicious werewolves have the little dude with hairy feet and his bearded dwarf friends trapped in a tree on the edge of a cliff; they're about to fall when a flock of eagles comes and whisks them away to safety. Keep those pictures in mind, and read this carefully:

> *Even the youths shall faint and be weary,*
> *And the young men shall utterly fall,*
> *But those who wait on the LORD*
> *Shall renew their strength;*
> *They shall mount up with wings like eagles,*
> *They shall run and not be weary,*
> *They shall walk and not faint.*
> ISAIAH 40:30-31

According to this passage, who becomes weak and tired?

Who are those who find renewed strength?

Consider your current circumstances. What is most wearisome to you in this season? What would it look like for God to renew your strength?

Like Gandalf and his Hobbit friends, as a blood-bought child of the King of kings, you have the right to cue the eagle anytime you are in need. Isaiah said even the youths will be weary and tired and even young men will fall in exhaustion. Young people have more energy than anyone, but Isaiah makes it clear that even they will run out of gas. When our spiritual batteries are running low, all we have to do is wait on the Lord and ask Him for strength. God promises that help will flow in response to such a request. That's what it means to cue the eagle.

In times of stress and fatigue, what keeps you from reaching out to God?

What counterfeit sources of strength are you
most likely to call on rather than God?

On a day-to-day basis, what does it look like to rely on
God's strength when you are out of strength?

EAGLE ALERT

The time to prepare for a marathon is not at the starting line, but long before race day approaches. So it is in your walk with Jesus, you should always train for the trial you're not yet in. At any given time, we're either in a trial, coming out of a trial, or coming upon a trial. So before you hit cruise control when life feels easy, remember there are things we can do to prepare ourselves for trials ahead. Undoubtedly, the most important thing we can do is to cultivate our relationship with Jesus. Read what Jesus had to say about what it means to stay connected to Him:

> I am the true vine, and My Father is the vinedresser. Every branch
> in Me that does not bear fruit He takes away; and every branch
> that bears fruit He prunes, that it may bear more fruit. You are
> already clean because of the word which I have spoken to you. Abide
> in Me, and I in you. As the branch cannot bear fruit of itself, unless
> it abides in the vine, neither can you, unless you abide in Me.
> I am the vine, you are the branches. He who abides in Me, and
> I in him, bears much fruit; for without Me you can do nothing.
> JOHN 15:1-5

What happens to a vine that becomes disconnected from the branch?
Why is this a fitting analogy of a life disconnected from Jesus?

Glance back at verse 4. What does Jesus instruct us to do?
What does it mean to "abide" in Jesus?

According to verse 5, what is the outcome for someone who
remains or abides in Jesus? What about those who attempt life apart
from Him? What steps can you take to draw closer to Him?

Our relationship with Jesus is the most important thing in this life. In times of feast or famine, heartache or joy, success or failure, there's nothing more valuable than knowing Him. Our degree of joy or lack of it will directly correlate with our level of intimacy with Jesus. Keep in mind, our relationship with Jesus shouldn't be viewed as some kind of insurance policy for hard times—it doesn't work that way. But if we invest in our relationship with Him and know Him well, He will be our greatest treasure. In doing so, we'll be more prepared to face the trials that come our way. The time to go deeper in your relationship with Christ is now.

Close your time by asking Jesus to abide with you.
Pray that this time today would lead to deeper intimacy with Him.

S.O.A.P.

Psalm 34:1-5

This week we spent time studying what it means to rely on God's strength rather than our own. As you spend time in this week's Scripture readings pay special attention to what God's Word has to say about this topic.

SCRIPTURE

OBSERVATION

APPLICATION

PRAYER

S.O.A.P.

Matthew 11:28-30

SCRIPTURE

OBSERVATION

APPLICATION

PRAYER

S.O.A.P.

Psalm 16:1-5

SCRIPTURE

OBSERVATION

APPLICATION

PRAYER

S.O.A.P.

Psalm 16:6-11

SCRIPTURE

OBSERVATION

APPLICATION

PRAYER

S.O.A.P.

Isaiah 26:3-4

SCRIPTURE

OBSERVATION

APPLICATION

PRAYER

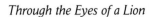

*Hard times are a passport that gives you permission
to go places you wouldn't get to any other way.*

WEEK 6
PAIN IS A MICROPHONE

START

Welcome to Session 6.

Last week we learned what it means to cue the eagle to rely on God's power and not our own. In this final lesson we'll discuss what it means to use pain as our microphone. Suffering isn't an obstacle to being used by God. It is an opportunity to be used like never before.

Have you ever been going through a hard time and been encouraged or comforted by someone who had a similar experience? If so, what happened?

In times of suffering, why is it sometimes helpful to be in touch with someone who has experienced a similar scenario?

Hard times are a passport that gives you permission to go places you wouldn't get to any other way. When we go through times of difficulty we have instant credibility with others who are suffering because they know we understand what it feels like to hurt. But it's up to us to decide if we're willing to use our experience with grief to help others.

Pray and ask God to use our time together.
After praying, watch the video teaching.

WATCH

DISCUSS

1. Levi said, "The hard things we go through are meant to be utilized to help others." Share one situation you have faced that you could use to help others.

2. We all have a variety of microphones (or platforms) where we have the opportunity to speak into other peoples' lives. In what areas or with whom has God given you influence?

3. In the video, Levi issued a challenge and said, "I dare you to live a life lit on fire by the Holy Spirit." What might that look like in your life?

4. How would you describe your level of comfort in sharing your past experiences of suffering to help others? If you have reservations, what are they?

5. Who in your life is going through a hard time? How might you use your unique history to reach out and encourage them?

6. Levi said, "God is able to take your misery and use it for ministry." What might this look like for you?

7. Share one lesson you've learned through this study.

Close your discussion with prayer.

PERSONAL STUDY 1
TURNING A MESS
INTO A MESSAGE

God doesn't cause bad things to happen, but He is sovereign and nothing happens outside His permission. The devil is the one ultimately responsible for evil. Sometimes it seems that life is out of control and more is given to us than we can bear. But everything is under God's control, and He leads us to breakthrough when we worship Him, no matter what we're going through. His endgame is to sabotage all your suffering and use what was meant for evil to accomplish His purposes (Gen. 50:20).

Read Romans 8:28.

**According to the above passage, what are the conditions
for all things working together for good?**

**How does it shape your life to love God and to
be called according to His purposes?**

**Can you think of a time when God brought good
from a bad situation? If so, what happened?**

REDEEMING OUR HEARTACHES

God's people need to be open to seeing how God redeems our heartaches. Enormous good can come to you when you let God use your heartache. It doesn't make the pain stop, but it does help heal your heart. It's not always easy to minister to someone who is hurting, sometimes we might just as soon not go there because it brings up painful emotions and memories. But if we push through and let God use our pain, we will always be glad we did—not just for the help it brings to others, but also for the peace it brings to our own heart.

What reservations do you have about making yourself available to others who are grieving?

We learn a lot about God, ourselves, and other people during times of suffering. What have you learned from your trials?

Think about your greatest hardship to date. What good would you like to see come from that experience? What is the next step you need to take to make that happen?

THE MORE WE HURT THE LOUDER WE BECOME

There is a connection between the strength of your pain and the volume of our voices to comfort. The more we hurt, the louder we become. This is why, though it's tempting, we must not be selfish with our pain. The lessons God teaches us in times of suffering are the lessons other people we encounter will desperately need. Consider the apostle Paul's words on comforting others:

Blessed be the God and Father of our Lord Jesus Christ, the Father of mercies and God of all comfort, who comforts us in all our tribulation, that we may be able to comfort those who are in any trouble, with the comfort with which we ourselves are comforted by God. For as the sufferings of Christ abound in us, so our consolation also abounds through Christ.

2 CORINTHIANS 1:3-5

According to Paul, who is the source of our comfort? Why does this matter?

What are we to do in response to the comfort God provides to us?

How might these verses comfort us even when we feel we have no comfort to offer?

How does the concept of "cue the eagle" or relying on God's strength rather than our own apply to comforting other people?

When you're going through a trial, it's easy to block out other people who are hurting. You might think, "I can't worry about them. I'm sorry other people have it bad, but I'm barely coping. I'm hanging on by a thread. I could hardly get out of bed this morning, so I just need to focus on me right now." No one will blame you. But if you are willing to step out in faith when you're in the fire yourself, you'll be astounded at how God will use you.

Why would God choose to use those who are hurting to comfort others?

What opportunities might come your way because of your hardship?

NOTHING IS WASTED

There are at least two reasons why you have influence when you're in a tough season of life. First, when you're going through a trial, people around you tend to get quieter. Secondly, when you're a Christian and you're going through a time of difficulty, you will notice that those around you who don't know Jesus Christ—especially those you've shared your faith with before—will lean in extra close. Their ears perk up. You've told them that Jesus is the anchor for your soul: He is the solid rock you can stand on. Now everything around you is giving away, and they want to find out if you're going to sink in the sand. If they do see your claims proven true, you'll find a greater willingness on their part to trust Christ in their own lives. Consider the words of the apostle Peter:

> *These trials will show that your faith is genuine. It is being tested as fire tests and purifies gold—though your faith is far more precious than mere gold. So when your faith remains strong through many trials, it will bring you much praise and glory and honor on the day when Jesus Christ is revealed to the whole world.*
> 1 PETER 1:7, NLT

In your experience, how do trials reveal what we really believe?

How have your trials impacted your faith?

What is the result when our faith remains strong during trials?

God wants to use your pain as a microphone. He can turn your mess into a message and your pain into a platform. He can turn your trials into your testimony. In God's economy, nothing is wasted. The only question is: Are you willing?

Pray that God would use your trials—past, present, and future—for His glory.

PERSONAL STUDY 2
RUN TOWARDS THE ROAR

I am fascinated by the way lions hunt. Lionesses actually do the bulk of the work. The fact that lionesses don't have a big recognizable mane actually helps them sneak up on whatever they are hunting. While the females stalk their prey from behind, the king of the jungle will come from the front and let loose a roar that can be heard up to five miles away. What the other animals don't know is the one who did the roaring is more bark than bite. So away they go—directly into the path of the waiting lioness. It's counterintuitive, but the right choice would be to override their emotions and run toward the roar. For some of us, using our pain as a microphone is scary, but Jesus commands those who follow Him to tell their stories. To do that we need to run to roar.

Read Luke 8:26-39.

Glance back at verse 27. What was the mental, physical, and emotional condition of the man in this account?

How would you describe the degree of this man's hardship?

Jesus healed the man by sending the demons that tormented him into a heard of pigs. According to verse 35, what was the man's condition after Jesus healed him? What difference did Jesus make?

After his healing, what did Jesus tell the man to do (v. 39)?

GO AND TELL

I can't think of a more dire situation than being demon-possessed, naked, and living in a cemetery. When Jesus encountered the man he'd been in this condition for a long time and had probably lost all hope of recovery. But Jesus stopped and did something remarkable—first, He treated the man like a human being, then He healed him. In an instant, Jesus made the man whole again.. Understandably, the man wanted to continue traveling with Jesus. But told him, "No, go back to your family, and tell them everything God has done for you" (v. 39).

Why do you think Jesus instructed the man to tell his story?

Who would've been lost if the man had kept his story to himself? Who could benefit from it?

What story is Jesus prompting you to tell?

Who might benefit from what you have to say?

What reservations do you have sharing your story? Why should you overcome these reservations?

If we want to use pain as our microphone we're going to have to face our fears and "run toward the roar." I can't tell you what God's will is for your life. There's no magic map, but I can tell you that you must not let fear play a part in your decision-making. You can't let fear silence the story God has given you. If God has ushered you through a time of grief, suffering, sadness, or disappointment then other people need to hear about it.

TIME TO ACT

Potential has a short shelf life. Like milk or produce, it doesn't keep forever. None of us know how much time we have left on this planet, so we need to make the most our time on this earth. You have a finite amount of time to act on the plans God has placed on your heart. Before we know it we'll be standing before God. James describes life this way:

> *How do you know what your life will be like tomorrow? Your life*
> *is like the morning fog—it's here a little while, then it's gone.*
> JAMES 4:14. NLT

Where is God leading you? What are your next steps?

What do you want to do with your time here on earth?

How can you use your life to make much of Jesus?

God wants you to shine brightly. Jesus said, " Let your good deeds shine out for all to see, so that everyone will praise your heavenly Father" (Matt. 5:16, NLT). God wants to use your hardships to touch other peoples' lives. Your pain shouldn't be wasted. But to live a life that brings glory to God, we are going to have to walk by faith and not by sight.

WALKING BY FAITH ALL THE WAY HOME

*So we are always confident, knowing that while we are at home in the
body we are absent from the Lord. For we walk by faith, not by sight.*
2 CORINTHIANS 5:6-7

How would you describe what it means to walk by faith and not by sight?

No one in this world is exempt from trouble and we will all have our share of trouble. But if we're willing, we have the opportunity to allow our hardships, pain, and struggles to drive us deeper into the arms of Jesus. As we grow in our relationship with Christ, we have the ability to experience peace in the fiercest storms. In the process, we have the privilege of being used by God to minister to other people who are suffering. But this life calls for a posture of faith. We can't pull it off on our own because God never intended for us to. We have to decide to walk by faith and trust that what God has said in His Word is true.

**What new insights have you learned over the last
six sessions that stand out to you?**

What has been most meaningful to you?

During the past six weeks, we've looked at what it means to view our circumstances through the eyes of a lion. We must not rely on the naked eye. What we think we see is not all that is there. There are unseen things. Spiritual things. Eternal things. To see life through the eyes of a lion we must utilize the telescope of faith, which will not only allow us to perceive the invisible—it will give us strength to do the impossible.

Thank God for all you've learned during your time in this study.

S.O.A.P.

1 Corinthians 2:1-5

This week we spent time studying what it means to use our experiences to help others. As you spend time in this week's Scripture readings pay special attention to what God's Word has to say about this topic.

SCRIPTURE

OBSERVATION

APPLICATION

PRAYER

S.O.A.P.

Matthew 28:18-19

SCRIPTURE

OBSERVATION

APPLICATION

PRAYER

S.O.A.P.

Isaiah 43:10-11

SCRIPTURE

OBSERVATION

APPLICATION

PRAYER

S.O.A.P.

Acts 4:13-20

SCRIPTURE

OBSERVATION

APPLICATION

PRAYER

S.O.A.P.

Psalm 34:1-3

SCRIPTURE

OBSERVATION

APPLICATION

PRAYER

LEADER GUIDE

HOW TO USE THIS LEADER GUIDE

Prepare to Lead

Before each session, go over the video teaching and read through the group discussion to prepare for the group meeting.

Familiarize yourself with the questions and begin thinking about how to best utilize these questions for the group you are leading. The following sections in the leader guide are given to help you facilitate the group well.

Main Point

This section summarizes the big idea of each session. Use this section to help focus your preparation and leadership during the group session.

Key Scriptures

Key passages of Scripture are listed for quick reference.

Considerations

The purpose of leading a group is to bring God's Word to the people in the group. This section is designed to help you consider and wrestle with the ideas in each session and to suggest ways to apply those truths to your group.

Pray

Use the prayer provided to close the leader guide or feel the freedom to lift up your own prayer.

TIPS FOR LEADING A SMALL GROUP

Prayerfully Prepare

Prepare for each group session with prayer. Ask the Holy Spirit to work through you and the group discussion as you point to Jesus each week through God's Word.

REVIEW the personal studies and the group sessions ahead of time.

PRAY for each person in the group.

Minimize Distractions

Do everything in your ability to help people focus on what's most important: connecting with God, with the Bible, and with one another.

Create a comfortable environment. If group members are uncomfortable, they'll be distracted and, therefore, not engaged in the group experience.

Take into consideration seating, temperature, lighting, refreshments, surrounding noise, and general cleanliness.

At best, thoughtfulness and hospitality show guests and group members they're welcome and valued in whatever environment you choose to gather. At worst, people may never notice your effort, but they're also not distracted.

Include Others

Your goal is to foster a community in which people are welcome just as they're, but are encouraged to grow spiritually. Always be aware of opportunities to include anyone who visits the group and invite new people to join your group.

Encourage Discussion

A good small-group experience has the following characteristics.

EVERYONE PARTICIPATES. Encourage everyone to ask questions, share responses, or read aloud.

NO ONE DOMINATES—NOT EVEN THE LEADER. Be sure your time speaking as a leader takes up less than half your time together as a group. Politely guide the discussion if anyone dominates.

NOBODY IS RUSHED THROUGH QUESTIONS. Don't feel that a moment of silence is a bad thing. People often need time to think about their responses to questions they've just heard or to gain courage to share what God is stirring in their hearts.

INPUT IS AFFIRMED AND FOLLOWED UP. Make sure you point out something true or helpful in a response. Don't just move on. Build community with follow-up questions, asking how other people have experienced similar things or how a truth has shaped their understanding of God and the Scripture you're studying. People are less likely to speak up if they fear that you don't actually want to hear their answers or that you're looking for only a certain answer.

GOD AND HIS WORD ARE CENTRAL. Opinions and experiences can be helpful, but God has given us the truth. Trust Scripture to be the authority and God's Spirit to work in peoples' lives. You can't change anyone, but God can. Continually point people to the Word and to active steps of faith.

Keep Connecting

Think of ways to connect with group members during the week. Participation during the group session always improves when members spend time connecting with one another outside the group sessions. The more people are comfortable with and involved in others' lives, the more they'll look forward to being together. When people move beyond being friendly to truly being friends who form a community, they come to each session eager to engage instead of merely attending.

SESSION 1
TURN OFF THE DARK

Main Point

One thing all people have in common is a desire to be happy. But it doesn't take long to realize this world is filled with pitfalls that can derail happiness. Evidence of darkness is everywhere we look, and we even see it in our own lives. Maybe it's in the form of loneliness, fear, depression, or guilt. Deep down, we know things aren't the way they are supposed to be, but we don't know how to fix it. Thankfully, in His mercy, God sent light into the darkness.

Key Scriptures

John 1:4   /   Matthew 1:23   /   2 Timothy 1:10

Considerations

Keep in mind members of your group are probably dealing with a variety of circumstances, and some are painful. You can encourage each group member by reminding them that Jesus can shine light into any situation, regardless of how severe it might seem.

Remember, some members will be more inclined to share than others, and that's OK. Ask each participant to think about the areas in their life in which they need Jesus to shine His light and to engage in this Bible study with those issues in mind.

Pray

Ask God to shine light in areas of darkness for each group member. Give thanks that Jesus is Immanuel or "God with us" and that He has not left us on our own but is an ever-present help. Pray each person will see evidence of the ways God is "turning off the dark" in specific areas in their lives.

SESSION 2
THE INVISIBLE WORLD

Main Point

On any given day, we have a choice about whether or not we are going to believe what our naked eye can see or believe what the Bible says about our spiritual realities. Most of the time, we shuffle along oblivious to what is actually happening. We drink our lattes and double-click our friends' pictures on Instagram, never giving thought to what is taking place in the spiritual realm. But when faced with overwhelming circumstances, we must be convinced that there is more to our reality than what we can see.

Key Scriptures

2 Corinthians 4:18   /   2 Kings 6:8-17

Considerations

Remember that each group member will have varying degrees of faith, depending on their spiritual maturity, background, and the season of life they are in. Nothing makes us question our faith more than when we are in the middle of a disaster and can't see the way out. But it's during times of testing when we decide what we really believe about God.

Help each person see that God is working even when we can't see what is happening. And it's during those times we learn to trust Him.

Pray

Ask God to increase the faith of each person in the group. Pray He will give them the strength they need to deal with their current circumstances. Ask God to increase their wisdom and knowledge of Him.

SESSION 3
HURTING WITH HOPE

Main Point

Hope is a powerful thing. The most important battle is the one you fight within, in your mind and heart, to not give up. At its most basic level, to have hope is to believe that something good is going to happen. That help is on the way. That it's not over yet, and no matter how dark it seems, there's going to be light at the end of the tunnel. Hope is a confident expectation that God will do what He has promised. When you have hope, gale-force winds can blow and waves can smash into the hull of your life, but you are buoyed by the belief that the best is yet to come. Brighter days are ahead. Hope quietly tells your heart that all is not lost, even as storms rage because our hope takes us directly to God.

Key Scriptures

Hebrews 6:19-20   /   1 Peter 1:21

Considerations

All of us experience times of grief and suffering. Believing in Jesus doesn't exempt us from emotional hardship, and being a Christian doesn't mean we won't shed tears during our time on earth. However, it does mean that when we do hurt, we do so with the knowledge that our best days are ahead of us and a time is coming when all sadness will come to an end.

Pray

Ask God to give the grace to fill each group member with hope. Pray God will renew a sense of hope and expectation each day and that each person will become increasingly convinced that God is worthy of trust and is faithful to keep His promises.

SESSION 4
THE HOPE OF HEAVEN

Main Point

As agonizing and painful as it can be, death is the ultimate upgrade for the believer: moving from the tent into the home Jesus has been preparing for you. When your earthly tent finally breaks down, you will open your eyes in the glory and majesty of heaven. Death is not the end of the road; it's just a bend in the road. Believers take their last breath here on earth and the next breath in the presence of God in heaven.

Key Scriptures

2 Corinthians 5:8   /   Luke 23:32-43

Considerations

Heaven is a real place that Christ-followers can look forward to with hope-filled expectation. But the reality is, many people, including Christians, have reservations and mixed emotions discussing this topic. You may have group members who have recently lost a loved one and are in a state of grief. Be sure to be sensitive to the different dynamics that group members may be going through.

Pray

Give thanks to God that believers in Christ will spend eternity with Him in heaven. Ask God to give an increased awareness to the brevity of life that motivates each person in the group to live with the expectation of heaven.

SESSION 5
CUE THE EAGLE

Main Point

Sometimes the things that we're hoping to happen take longer than anticipated or transpire in a way that leads to disappointment. During times of waiting, disappointment, or grief, we're prone to become weary. But it's during those times we learn to "Cue the Eagle," meaning we learn to rely on God's strength rather than our own.

Key Scriptures

Luke 24:13-35   /   Isaiah 40:31

Considerations

Some group members will have a closer relationship with Jesus than others. Emphasize that our relationship with Jesus is the most important thing in this life. In times of feast or famine, heartache or joy, success or failure, there's nothing more valuable than knowing Him. Our degree of joy or lack of it will directly correlate with our level of intimacy with Jesus. Keep in mind, our relationship with Jesus shouldn't be viewed as some kind of insurance policy for hard times—it doesn't work that way. But if we invest in our relationship with Him and know Him well He will be our greatest treasure. In doing so, we'll be more prepared to face the trials that come our way. The time to go deeper in your relationship with Christ is now.

Pray

Ask God to give each group member the desire to prioritize their relationship with Jesus above everything else. Pray that they will learn to rely on God's strength and not their own. Give thanks to God for His grace that we may know Him.

SESSION 6
PAIN IS A MICROPHONE

Main Point

God doesn't cause bad things to happen, but He is sovereign and nothing happens outside His permission. The devil is the one ultimately responsible for evil. Sometimes it seems that life is out of control and more is given to us than we can bear. But everything is under God's control, and He leads us to breakthrough when we worship Him, no matter what we're going through. His endgame is to sabotage all your suffering and use what was meant for evil to accomplish His purposes (Gen. 50:20).

Key Scriptures

Romans 8:28   /   2 Corinthians 1:3-5

Considerations

Some group members may feel ambivalent about using their pain as a platform to serve others and that is understandable. Offer encouragement by reminding them they aren't alone in their struggle. No one in this world is exempt from trouble and we will all have our share of trouble. But if we're willing, we have the opportunity to allow our hardships, pain, and struggles to drive us deeper into the arms of Jesus. As we grow in our relationship with Christ, we have the ability to experience peace in the fiercest storms. In the process, we have the privilege of being used by God to minister to other people who are suffering.

Pray

Give thanks to God for the new truths learned during the last six weeks of study. Pray that God will lead each member to use their experiences in a way that brings Him glory. Ask God to empower each of them to look at their circumstances through the lens of faith.